essential careers™

A CAREER IN
COMPUTER GRAPHICS AND DESIGN

JOE GREEK

ROSEN
PUBLISHING

NEW YORK

INTRO

Today, graphic designers often work long hours without ever leaving their computers. As technology progresses, however, they may have to adapt to new work standards and environments.

DUCTION

I t seems that in every direction one turns, there is good chance of finding an example of graphic design. The label on a tube of Chapstick, a book cover, or the manufacturer's logo on the tag of a shirt are all created by graphic designers. For members of this professional community, creative and artistic qualities are just as important as being able to envision a design through the eyes of a customer. Famed graphic designer Milton Glaser once said, "There are three responses to a piece of design—yes, no, and WOW! Wow is the one to aim for."

Graphic designers have to make their work visually appealing while at the same time informative and memorable. Package designers, for example, have to create designs that are capable of grabbing the attention of a potential customer. Then the packaging must explain to the customer what is inside and why it's so different from the similar product sitting next to it on the shelf.

The graphic design profession has greatly changed since the days when designers did all of their work strictly by hand, without the aid of a computer. Today, most graphic design work can be carried out from concept to final product by using a keyboard and mouse. There is an array of different software programs that can transform rough photographs into beautiful works of art, a business or product into a recognized brand, and rough concepts into seamless video. The field continues to experience change, as the technology that drives graphic design today will change with time—and with that, so will the profession as a whole. With that understanding in mind, it is easy to see that creating and maintaining a successful career will require a desire to continue learning.

Graphic design can be a very rewarding career, both financially and creatively. For the artist, it is an opportunity to have a job that is also a passion. Additionally, graphic designers can work almost anywhere, including in a city such as San Francisco or from the comfort of a house in rural Idaho. Such benefits mean graphic design is a popular career, and that popularity, in turn, means that the industry is very competitive. Finding a job, any job, can be very difficult when the economy is floundering, and to be able to find a place within the profession of one's choice requires determination and hard work.

Unfortunately, there is no guaranteed path that will lead someone directly to a high-paying job within the graphic design field. However, aspiring graphic designers can prepare to improve their chances of finding that dream job while they are still in middle or high school. By learning all they can about the industry, and gaining practical, hands-on experience with some of the most popular computer design programs on the market today, prospective graphic designers can turn hard work and creativity into a rewarding career.

chapter 1

AREAS OF GRAPHIC DESIGN

Choosing the right career path when seeking a job in graphic design can seem intimidating at first. However, simply looking around a room can be reassuring, as it reveals just how many different options there are in the field. Newspapers, toothpaste containers, websites, and business cards each display a designer's fingerprints.

In the past, designers often worked with pens and paints, but today they work primarily with keyboards, computer mice, and styluses. Therefore, a designer no longer has to be a master at illustrating by hand. For the most part, both print and digital designers rely on the use of computer programs.

While there are a variety of niche jobs in the graphic design industry, there are a number of positions that are especially popular with job-seekers in this creative field. These include print publication designer, packaging designer, advertising and marketing designer, web designer, and multimedia designer.

PRINT PUBLICATION DESIGNERS

Readers who flip through the pages of a newspaper, an issue of *Rolling Stone* magazine, or the print version of a book may not realize that graphic designers played a major role in creating these publications. Traditional print publications depend on their designers for a number of reasons. To begin with, a publication designer must use his or her knowledge of size

What is shown on a computer screen may not always look the same in print. Here, a designer compares printed color samples to the digital images on the screen.

specifications and printing guidelines to lay out text, images, and graphics. For example, a designer who is working on two pages that share one image, known as a spread, will have to lay out the material so that it does not become distorted by the space between the two facing pages, which is called the gutter.

Print publication designers also must have a working knowledge of color formatting. Most computer screens and graphic design programs show colors in the Red-Green-Blue (RGB) color model. However, if the images are left in RGB mode, the printed version may come out darkened because printers lack the ability to produce the amount of colors that can be shown on a monitor's display. Therefore, publication designers work on projects using the Cyan-Magenta-Yellow-Black (CMYK) color model, which allows them to see on screen exactly how an image will appear in print. Since many publications offer print and digital products, designers have to keep color formatting in mind as they go back and forth.

Finally, publication designers have to ensure that their work is both visually appealing and easy for the reader to navigate. The pages of a newspaper, for example, tend to be laid out in columns so that readers are less likely to lose their place as they scan their eyes from left to right. Designers also have to make sure that pages are not too cluttered and that related images and text stay together. Additionally, the front page or cover of a publication is usually designed to be eye-catching so that potential buyers will become curious about what is on the inside pages.

PACKAGING DESIGNERS

Walking through the aisles of a grocery store reveals examples of the type of work that a packaging designer produces on a daily basis. Packaging designers are responsible for the designs of numerous types of packaging, including boxes, bottles, cartons, and packets. Their job responsibilities can range from creating only the illustrations and graphics to designing the entire product package.

When packaging designers begin a project, they must keep several key points in mind. First, a package has to protect its contents from being damaged. The packaging used for food products, for example, has to be constructed under strict guidelines that prevent the contents from becoming exposed to bacteria or other germs that could cause contamination.

Second, packaging designers need to have a thorough understanding of the production process and the different types of materials that are used, such as glass, plastics, paper, and wood. Due to the cost of packaging materials and recycling concerns,

To consumers, great packaging design creates brand awareness and triggers an instant recognition or memory of the product. Most people, for example, quickly recognize the bright packaging and labels on ketchup and mustard bottles.

MILTON GLASER

American graphic designer Milton Glaser rose to commercial and artistic fame when he cofounded Pushpin Studios in 1954. Trained as a classical fine artist, Glaser produced work that did not conform to the standard of graphic design at the time, which consisted of direct and realistic illustrations. Instead, Glaser's works were more simplistic in design and often used bright colors. One of his most widely recognized designs that demonstrates the power of simplicity is the iconic "I Love New York" logo, which he created in 1977. To this day, the logo is sold in shops across New York City on an assortment of products, including T-shirts, key chains, and bumper stickers.

Throughout the 1960s and 1970s, Glaser's art was featured on numerous music albums and posters. Original prints of his 1966 poster for the album *Bob Dylan's Greatest Hits* often sell for hundreds of dollars at auction. Glaser's influence also spread to print publications. In 1968, he cofounded *New York* magazine, where he served as the president and design director until 1977. The magazine, which is still in publication, resulted in a number of imitations across the planet.

Considered a groundbreaker by his contemporaries, Glaser strived to create art that was unfamiliar. In a 1999 interview with *CSD (Chartered Society of Designers) Magazine*, Glaser remarked, "I have always thought that in order to stay interested in what you are doing, to some extent you have to operate in the realm of what you do not know; that professionalism moves you forward towards a kind of rote understanding, in the same way that academic activity leads you towards academic, or repeatable ideas."

designers have to be mindful about what they use, how much material is needed, and how it can affect the environment.

Finally, package designers have to make products visually appealing to consumers, especially when there are competing products on the same shelf. The visual appearance of a package for marketing is important for clients because it can create brand recognition. For example, the packaging for some products, such as SPAM meat products and Campbell's Soup, has rarely changed over the past several decades because generations of shoppers instantly recognize the products by design and graphics.

Packaging designers work closely with clients to determine how they envision their products to be marketed on shelves. To begin, the designer often works with traditional design tools such as pens and paints to create rough sketches for the client to critique. Next, the designer may use programs such as Adobe Illustrator to create digital illustrations of the artwork used for the package. Additionally, they often use computer-aided design (CAD) programs to create 3-D designs of the packaging that other members of the production process then use to construct the actual package that sits on the shelf.

ADVERTISING AND MARKETING DESIGNERS

Aside from creating a product or providing a service, businesses have to deliver messages to their potential consumers in order to make a profit. Large companies and small businesses alike use advertising and marketing techniques to make their products known to the public. Designers who work in the offices of an advertising or marketing firm are commonly referred to as "in-house designers."

Graphic designers in this field may have the opportunity to work in several different media areas, including print, web, and television. Designers may also create graphics, digital animations, and videos for the web and/or broadcast television commercials. Regardless of the media, graphic designers at marketing and advertising firms generally have some contact with clients in order to create advertisements that are placed in print publications or on websites.

Depending on the size of the company, a graphic designer may focus on one creative service or in several different areas. Full-service advertising agencies provide clients with a wide variety of services, including branding, which involves making a product or company distinct. Branding a business includes the creation of logos and developing recognizable themes and graphics that are used in different advertising and marketing services.

Whereas an advertising agency builds a company's recognition through branding, marketing departments utilize existing brands to increase sales. Graphic designers in a marketing department focus on creating promotional materials found inside stores, such as coupons, catalogs, and cardboard displays that use preexisting logos. Designers also create flyers that are found inside newspapers and that many people call "junk mail," which is advertisements sent directly to a person's home.

WEB DESIGNERS

Construction of a website revolves around two main categories—"front end" and "back end." The front end is what a user sees on his or her computer or mobile device screen. The back end of a website refers to the inner workings or coding that is not visible to the viewer and is typically handled by a web developer. In essence, a developer is responsible for making a website work, whereas the graphic designer ensures that a site is visually appealing.

Front-end website designers spend a lot of time using software programs such as Photoshop and Fireworks to create

A website's audience is no longer limited to individuals at home or the office. Web designers now have to take mobile devices into consideration when working on a project.

drafts of how the website should look. They work closely with developers to make adjustments to designs in order to accommodate the actual coding of the site. Since the web is accessed by people using a variety of different-sized screens, designers have to work with an understanding that what is displayed on a desktop computer may appear different on a smartphone.

The ability for a user to interact with a website is another aspect that web designers have to take into consideration.

Designers may work with a site's user interface, which is considered a subsegment of front-end design. Web designers who work on a user interface are often required to have knowledge of some kind of coding, such as HTML, CSS, JavaScript, and PHP, in addition to their graphic design skills. While it is debatable as to whether or not a designer should also focus on coding, more and more employers are searching for designers that have an understanding of basic coding skills.

DIGITAL GRAPHICS AND MULTIMEDIA DESIGNERS

In a 2013 article about the state of print design that appeared in *Graphic Design USA* magazine, David LeDrew, art director of the digital photo manipulation company Photozig, said, "With mobile devices in almost every hand, print has a much smaller role today compared to forty years ago. The days of the large *Life* magazine are in the past. I do not think print will ever die, but when most want to see what just happened right now, it is hard to compete."

Utilizing the web as a marketing tool makes it possible for businesses to connect with and engage consumers more frequently than traditional print. Because of the impact the Internet has on businesses, the need for computer graphics artists—commonly referred to as digital graphic designers or multimedia designers—who are experienced in creating material for the web is also growing.

Graphic designers are not limited to using only a keyboard and mouse. A graphics tablet, which acts as a digital pen and paper, makes it easier to create free-form visuals.

Digital graphic designers are responsible for creating a variety of material for the web, including infographics, such as charts and graphs, and advertisements for websites. Additionally, digital graphic designers play an important role in the creation of e-books, apps, and computer/online games. Designers who primarily work with digital computer graphics rely on a thorough knowledge of the industry's software, as well as how their designs will appear on different devices.

Digital animation is another area of graphic design that has grown as a result of the web. Combining an array of media—including text, video, photos, and graphics—into a cohesive, animated presentation is the job of a multimedia designer. These individuals use computer graphics and elements of many kinds to produce short animated films that entertain viewers while also showcasing a company's products and services.

chapter 2

WORK ENVIRONMENTS

There are many types of businesses that employ graphic designers, from very small family-run shops to companies that have thousands of employees. The work environment will vary from employer to employer. Some offices are quiet and laid back, while others are loud and busy with ringing phones and staff members shouting across the room. Companies also require different amounts and types of work performed by their designers. The following covers several of the most common work environments that a designer fits into, as well as what can be expected on any given work day.

ADVERTISING AGENCIES

Advertising agencies are responsible for promotional materials that appear across a variety of media platforms, including television, radio, print publications, and the web. The number of employees that an advertising agency has can range anywhere from less than twenty to more than one hundred. Additionally, the size of an advertising agency can vary greatly depending on where it is located. A successful agency in a highly populated city, for example, will generally have more potential clients than an agency in a smaller community, and will therefore require more staff. Many advertising agencies employ their own graphic designers, while others contract with design studios that employ freelance designers.

At a large agency, designers can expect to be around a variety of employees with different jobs. Being able to work well with other people and personalities is important to succeed in a large office.

One of the benefits of working for a larger agency is that positions are generally focused on a specific aspect of the production process. Large advertising firms tend to be divided into different departments, such as design, editorial, marketing, and administration. At large agencies with employees who specialize in one aspect of design, such as print media or digital animation, the jobs tend to be competitive. Employers may prefer hiring candidates who have a strong background in certain design roles, rather than a designer who has worked in several different positions.

Smaller firms, on the other hand, often have one person covering many different jobs and may want designers who can

DRESS CODES

Businesses often require their employees to follow a dress code. Dress codes are rules for what can and cannot be worn in the workplace. Because every work environment is unique, they vary from office to office. Businesses where the staff does not frequently interact with clients may allow workers to wear casual clothing, which could consist of jeans, athletic shoes, and T-shirts. Offices where clients regularly visit may ask their employers to wear more formal clothing, such as dresses, dress shirts, and ties.

For many businesses that employ graphic designers, however, "business casual" is the required clothing style. Business casual falls between casual and formal (suit and tie). Exactly what clothing fits into this category is debatable. According to *Forbes* reporter Renee Sylvestre-Williams, who asked readers what they considered business casual, "There seemed to be agreement on: 'For men: trousers/khakis, and a shirt with a collar. For women: trousers/knee-length skirt and a blouse or shirt with a collar. No jeans. No athletic wear.'"

handle several different design-related projects. For example, a small advertising agency may need a graphic designer who is experienced with designing logos and creating short animated movies for a client's website.

PUBLISHERS

Working for a publication such as a newspaper or magazine, or a publishing house that creates hard-copy books and e-books, requires an in-depth attention to organization and the ability to meet strict deadlines. Designers who work for such publications tend to specialize in the areas of layout and typography, and spend most of their time in front of a computer screen. Depending on the size of the publication, designers can expect to work closely with photographers, editors, copy editors, and ad salespeople.

Newspapers, particularly those printed daily, are created under intense deadlines that each department has to meet. Many employees, including designers, end up working late hours because breaking news events may occur that have to be placed into the publication at the last moment. Usually taking notes from an editor, the designer has to place each story and accompanying photo(s) within the proper section of the paper and in order of the article's "newsworthiness." The work that a designer does for a magazine is similar to that for a newspaper. However, magazines and book publishers usually allow more room for creativity when it comes to design. Designers working in these environments may also have to perform touch-up work on photos using editing programs such as Photoshop.

Publication designers also typically work with reporters/writers, editors, and copy editors to ensure that all the necessary material fits into the publication. This can involve asking an editor or writer to cut or add text when space becomes an issue. When the layout of a publication is completed and reviewed, the designer sends the file to press, which means sending it to a department or company that then prints the publication.

With the increased use of mobile technology, the role of newspaper and magazine designers is also evolving as more traditional print publications move toward digital distribution. Many employers are now looking for designers that understand web coding and mobile app technologies.

INTERVIEW WITH A TELECOMMUTING DESIGNER

Barry Cantrell is an interactive designer for Mother Nature Network (MNN). His responsibilities include making infographics and animated videos for the MNN website, using Adobe Photoshop, Illustrator, After Effects, and SoundBooth. As a remote worker, he spends most of his time in his home office, although he interacts daily with other staff.

What are the benefits of working from home?

I love not getting called into meetings or getting distracted by people around me. It's a lot easier to focus on my work. Also, I am able to save a lot of money on gas and car insurance because I don't spend much time driving to an office.

How do you manage to stay productive?

With my job, I don't have concrete hours, but I decided to work concrete hours anyway. I think you need a solid structure when it comes to work schedules. . . .I also limit myself on how much time I surf the web. Some days, I feel less motivated than others, so I set goals for myself. I'll tell myself, "I'm going to work on this project for an hour and then reward myself with a few minutes of playing a videogame or getting on YouTube."

What advice do you have for young people that are interested in graphic design?

You don't have to be the best designer, but you do have to hit deadlines. Also, get broad experience. Employers that I've talked to or worked with want well-rounded designers who know how to design for the web and animation.

"In-House" or "Remote"

The type of work environment graphic designers may experience also depends on their work status. Where they work depends on whether they are "in-house" employees or work remotely, from a location other than their employer's base of operations. In-house graphic designers work wherever their employer is based, whether it is a retail store, a manufacturer, or a marketing firm. Remote designers can work just about any place; the Internet has made it possible for many graphic designers to do their work without even leaving their house. Also referred to as telecommuters, remote employees typically work from a home office or out of a rented office space. This makes it possible for employers to hire individuals who live a long distance away or even out-of-state.

Businesses often hire telecommuters because it can help them save money and office space. Using remote workers also allows employers to hire qualified individuals whom they might not be able to find locally. Additionally, according to a 2013 article by Dinah Wisenberg Brin for the Society for Human Resource Management, "Supporters cite the advantages, including greater flexibility and work/life balance for employees, savings on commuting time and costs, environmental and energy conservation, lower real estate expenses for companies and, with good management practices, better productivity."

The idea of working from home may sound appealing to many graphic designers, but employers still require their telecommuters to be productive. Remote workers still have to maintain communication with their bosses and coworkers through e-mail, instant messenger, telephone, and videoconference. Not all telecommuters have the option of making up their own work schedules either. Remote workers are usually expected to work the same amount of hours as in-office staff. Working from home can also be difficult for individuals who

Establishing a daily routine is often necessary in order for remote workers to avoid becoming distracted at home. Employers and clients expect results regardless of whether a designer works in an office or bedroom.

are easily distracted. Without having a boss over their shoulder, some employees may end up spending too much time surfing the web instead of doing their work. This can often be seen in the quality of an individual's work or productivity. Remote workers are expected to contribute just as much to their company as they would if they worked in the office.

FREELANCE WORKERS

Considered their own boss, freelance graphic designers also run their own business. Like remote designers, freelance workers have a large amount of freedom and control over their work environment. They make their own work schedule and choose their own dress code. They also choose their own clients and what projects they undertake.

However, with the added freedom of being a freelance designer there also come additional responsibilities. For one, freelance designers have to find their own potential clients and market their skills. To do this, they rely on word of mouth and recommendations from satisfied clients. Additionally, some freelance designers market their services on the web through social media and personal websites. This can involve putting in several

Creative minds often enjoy being in full control of the work they do. Freelance graphic designers are able to decide which clients and type of projects they want to pursue.

hours a week networking with other designers and potential clients online in order to find work.

A full-time freelance designer must work hard to build a good reputation. Being communicative with clients and maintaining financial records are two aspects of this.

Freelance designers also play the administrative role that secretaries, accountants, and other staff do in a traditional office setting. For example, a freelance worker has to keep track of all work-related income and expenses in order to properly file taxes. While freelance designers have the ability to become very successful at what they do, they nonetheless have to be hard workers.

Perhaps even more than in-house and remote graphic designers, freelance designers have to meet deadlines, as their reputation—and livelihood—depend on it. No one wants to hire a worker who cannot deliver good work on time. The downside is that even if a freelance designer does a great job and meets all due dates, there is no guarantee that work will come in regularly.

chapter 3

Tools and Software of the Trade

Today's graphic designer no longer relies on colored pencils and rulers to create eye-catching advertisements. A computer is now the artist's palette, and software provides the paint and brush. The most commonly used graphic design programs are created by Adobe Systems Incorporated. There are also several alternatives to many of the Adobe programs, but they are not as popular.

Operating Systems

One of the biggest debates in the graphic design industry is what computer operating system is the best. Currently, there are three operating systems that are boasted as the most frequently used around the world—Windows, Mac, and Linux. Within the workplace, a designer should only expect to encounter two of the three operating systems.

Web and computer programmers often use Linux, which according to results from a January 2014 survey by NetMarketShare.com is used by only 1.6 percent of computer owners. The Mac and Windows operating systems, on the other hand, are the popular choice for graphic designers. Though Mac users account for only 7.68 percent of computer owners compared to Windows' 90.72 percent, the Mac system is still very popular within the industry. Since the 1980s, the Mac has held a reputation for being the

The Mac operating system is run on Apple's line of desktop computers, laptops, and tablets. Knowing how to navigate the Mac operating system is often a desired skill by graphic design employers.

artist's personal computer. In a 2010 *Computer Weekly* column, Faisal Alani wrote, "Macs appear to be cooler/ trendier but they are also a better fit for designers. Apple has carved out a reputation for being the 'alternative' choice for those that see themselves as an individual, which is what art is all about."

However, Mac's reputation as the "cool" operating system doesn't necessarily mean that it is better than Windows. In fact, both operating systems can generally run the same programs that are used by designers. Additionally, many people prefer Windows machines because they are more affordable. In any event, designers should know the basics of using both operating systems.

PHOTO EDITING

One of the most popular graphics editing programs in use today is Adobe Photoshop. It is a graphic creation and editing program, which can be used for a wide variety of purposes. Introduced in 1990,

A photograph may need to be enhanced or altered to fit into a project or to suit a client's needs. The ability to edit or manipulate digital photographs is an important part of most graphic design jobs.

Photoshop has since become one of the primary programs used by most graphic designers.

In print media, such as magazines, Photoshop is often used by graphic designers to edit or "retouch" photographs. Retouching involves using various Photoshop functions to balance colors, remove or add visual elements, or to enhance and diminish parts of the original photograph. In fashion and health magazines, in particular, retouching has become a controversial practice because altered photographs of models tend to present a "perfected" or "ideal" body image. Aside from retouching photographs, Photoshop can be used to design countless print projects, including business cards, invitations, posters, bumper stickers, flyers, and packaging artwork.

Photoshop is not limited to working with photographs. The most recent releases of the program provide users with video editing tools that allow common video formats, such as MOV, FLV, and AVI, to be manipulated. Additionally, Photoshop 14.1 introduced functions that allow designers to work with three-dimensional (3-D) printing files. Three-dimensional printing is the process of designing an object with software that can then be printed in layers by a special printer that uses plastics, metals, and even chocolate to produce a 3-D product.

Photoshop has very few rivals that come close to even competing as an alternative for graphic designers. It can be used for simple projects such as event flyers and for designing large projects such as billboard ads. Additionally, Adobe provides a free, simplified version of the program for smartphone and tablet owners called Photoshop Express.

ILLUSTRATION

When it comes to computer-drawn illustrations, Adobe Illustrator is the go-to program. In many ways, Illustrator functions similarly to Photoshop. Graphic designers can use

Illustrators used to draw their projects using colored pencils and tools such as rulers. Today, they generally use illustration software and devices like a graphics tablet.

Illustrator to create a variety of projects that can be done with Photoshop, such as logos, business cards, and packaging art.

Though designers can manipulate digital photographs using Illustrator, the program's primary function is its ability to create vector graphics. Unlike digital photographs that are also known as raster graphics—meaning they are made up of a certain number of pixels—Illustrator is used to mathematically draw vector graphics that are not constrained to a determined amount of pixels. Because vector graphics are not made up of a specific number of pixels, the size of the graphic can be drastically changed without losing any quality. A raster graphic, on the other hand, would become blurry if the size of the image was increased because the individual pixels would become more visible.

Illustrator can be used for a number of projects. Equipped with a stylus, an artist can hand-draw illustrations directly into a computer. For many artists, such as comic book illustrators, the program has replaced the use of traditional

ADOBE EXPERT CERTIFICATION

The job market for graphic designers is competitive. From the stacks of job applications, an employer will choose candidates based on their education and work history. Because of the competitive nature of the graphic design industry, any advantage can become the deciding factor between candidates. One way to stand out from the rest of the competition is to become an Adobe Certified Expert (ACE).

To become an ACE, a designer can take one of the official Adobe exams to demonstrate proficiency in one or more of the programs. There are three different types of ACE exams to choose from. The first type of exam is the "single product certification" option, which covers one specific program, such as InDesign or Photoshop. The second option is the "specialist certification" exam. This exam focuses on the specific design mediums of web, print, and video. The final type of exam is called "master certification." Master certification demonstrates an individual's expertise of an entire Adobe suite collection of programs. The Creative Design collection, for example, includes InDesign, Photoshop, Illustrator, and Acrobat.

The ACE tests are given in person at offices around the world. The exams consist of multiple-choice questions where the taker must apply his or her knowledge of a program to real-world situations. Adobe offers preparation guides for each program on its website. A certification does not last forever, though. When a program has been upgraded, Adobe will require individuals to take a new exam to renew their ACE status.

colored pencils and pens. Illustrator can also be used to add illustrations to video projects and digital photographs. Additionally, 3-D designs can be created with the program. Because most companies use the Adobe products, there are few alternatives to Illustrator in the workplace. However, there are many similar programs that individuals can use at home, including Corel Draw, Inkscape, Sketch, and iDraw.

Desktop Publishing

Page layout has come a long way from the days of Johannes Gutenberg's printing press. Today's most-used desktop publishing programs are Adobe InDesign, QuarkXPress, and Pages for Mac. These programs have similar functions and abilities to produce creative page designs that are used for a variety of projects, including brochures, pamphlets, books, newsletters, newspapers, and magazines. Whereas Photoshop and Illustrator are primarily used to edit and create graphic images and illustrations, desktop publishing software is mainly used to arrange graphics, video, and text together.

In the past, desktop publishing programs were generally used for the production of printed material. Today, however, they are also frequently used to produce digital publications, such as books and magazines that can be read on tablets. Furthermore, there are also several low-cost and free alternatives that can be found online for producing basic layouts for projects such as newsletters that don't require all the functions of the more complex programs.

InDesign, like other Adobe products, is the most widely used layout program among graphic designers. Beyond being able to simply combine text and images into a page, InDesign can work with several different media types, including video, image, flash, and audio, to create colorful projects for the web and devices such as smartphones. While InDesign cannot be

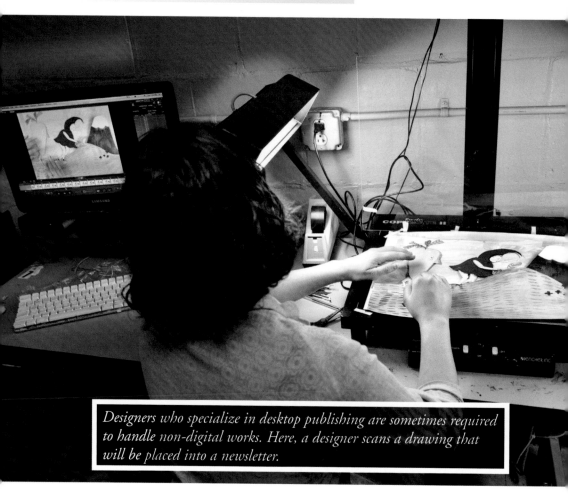

Designers who specialize in desktop publishing are sometimes required to handle non-digital works. Here, a designer scans a drawing that will be placed into a newsletter.

used to create every part of a project as well as specific Adobe programs can, it has the ability to take those individual pieces to make captivating, interactive projects that display the growing possibilities of desktop publishing.

Animation and Multimedia

The technologies created as a result of the web have created new types of jobs within the graphic design industry. Digital

FONT MANAGEMENT

Graphic designers who create products for print should know how to prepare and handle their digital components. For example, there are countless numbers of fonts available to designers. Without the aid of font management software, keeping track of them can become a difficult task. Software such as FontExplorer X Pro and MainType allows users to organize, activate, deactivate, and preview fonts. Fonts play a vital role in design, and some large companies even have employees that specialize in font management.

videos, animation, advertisements, and games are just a few of the new types of web products that graphic designers are involved with. To create these projects, which go beyond 2-D imagery to include audio and even interactive elements, graphic designers use animation and video editing programs.

For web use, Adobe Flash is used to create animated vector graphics and to add animation to raster graphics as well. Flash can be used to create interactive, animated advertisements and even games for web browsers. However, the use of Flash files on websites is declining because the newer web coding language HTML5 doesn't require devices to have the program Flash Player installed. Still, Flash projects can be converted to HTML5-readable files. Other animation programs that are popular with designers include Maya, Blender, and FlipBook.

Combining animation and visual elements from different sources is called "compositing." This practice is often used in the post-production process for creating films and videos for the web and traditional film. One of the most popular programs used by designers for compositing is Adobe After Effects. This program allows users to create and modify videos using multiple layers. These different layers can consist of different types of media, such as audio, animation, and text. Aside from After Effects, some companies use NUKE or Digital Fusion among other compositing software choices.

WEB DESIGN

Programs involving web design tend to fall under the responsibility of web designers. However, some employers prefer job candidates that have at least a basic understanding of web design. Websites are created from different types of coding, including HTML5, PHP, and CSS. Adobe Dreamweaver, Notepad++, and Komodo Edit are just a few of the most well known web coding programs. Moreover, there are also popular website creation services, such as WordPress and Squarespace, which provide predesigned templates that don't require a thorough coding knowledge to produce professional-looking sites.

chapter 4

PREPARING FOR A CAREER IN GRAPHIC DESIGN

There's no better time than the present for a high school or middle school student to begin figuring out how to achieve career goals. Becoming a professional graphic designer requires a dedication to learning the tools of the trade, understanding the audience, and a desire to continually improve upon one's skills and abilities. The following sections provide a basic overview and tips for transitioning from high school student to college student and eventually to professional graphic designer.

HIGH SCHOOL COURSES

Anyone who is interested in becoming a professional graphic designer should consider pursuing a bachelor's degree in graphic design or a related field. Students in high school may wonder what options they have in this regard that will allow them to begin preparing for the future. The fact of the matter is that many high schools offer courses that will point prospective graphic designers in the right direction.

To begin with, students interested in graphic design should take as many art- and design-related courses their school has to offer. Art classes that involve actual hands-on work, such as drawing and painting, will help develop and improve a student's ability to design freehand. Being able to sketch an idea or rough draft of a design can come in handy when working face-to-face with clients or a team. Courses in art history can also help to broaden one's knowledge of the different styles of art. Some schools may even offer computer graphics courses or classes that cover CAD design.

Future graphic designers should be careful not to limit themselves to art courses, however. Graphic designers often have to rely on a variety of skills in the workplace that are not directly related to art or design. Consider taking business courses such as marketing, finance, and management. Additionally, classes in writing and public speaking can also be beneficial when working in team environments that require giving presentations.

GOING TO COLLEGE

According to the U.S. Bureau of Labor Statistics, employers generally look for graphic designers who

have a bachelor's degree. Not to say that a college degree is mandatory, but the BLS also estimates that the job growth for graphic designers from 2012 to 2022 will be slower than average for all occupations. As employment within the industry

Taking art courses is a great way to become better prepared for college and beyond. An understanding of art outside of the computer screen will only help improve one's eye for detail and appreciation for visual design.

continues to be competitive, entry-level job seekers with a degree will have an advantage.

How do people find a degree program that meets their career goals? First, they should talk with their school counselor. Part of a counselor's job is to provide assistance to students seeking education beyond high school. They should be able to help come up with a list of schools that offer design

Aside from personal research online, talking to a guidance counselor may help a student determine if graphic design is the career he or she truly desires to pursue.

degrees. Next, students should examine the courses that are offered by schools they are interested in. Read descriptions of the classes and learn more about the credibility of the programs offered. As they study each school and the required courses, students can ask themselves the following questions:

- What is the primary emphasis of the program? Print, web, video?

- Do I have a choice of electives?
- Is it possible to obtain a minor or double major?
- Does the school offer internship or job-placement assistance?
- Do the offered courses prepare students for graduate study?
- If the school doesn't offer a bachelor's degree, will the courses transfer to a four-year school?

Aside from the actual classes that are taught, students should also research the faculty. Most colleges provide background information on their teachers, including education and work history. This type of information can usually be found within an institution's course catalog or website. Determine whether or not the instructors have strong backgrounds within the graphic design industry. What sort of experience do they have that will be beneficial? Also, find out how many instructors there are within a program. For example, a program that has only one or two instructors may not provide enough diversity of design skills and experience. Additionally, take into consideration the student-to-teacher ratio. Programs with a large amount of students may indicate that the faculty will be unable to provide adequate attention to individual student needs.

Once the choice of schools has been narrowed down, it is time to schedule tours of the campuses, if possible. Seeing the institutions firsthand will help students determine which one is right for them. While visiting a campus, people should try to speak with faculty and students to get answers to the questions they have. Find out if current students enjoy the program and what they like and dislike about it. A tour of classrooms can help determine if a school provides the most up-to-date design tools, computers, and software.

Determining which school is best may sound daunting. Just remember that there are numerous programs with

DESIGN CONTESTS

In the graphic design industry, it can be difficult to stand out from the rest of the crowd. Fortunately, competitions provide an opportunity for designers to show off their mastery of color, detail, and ability to balance message and art. There are countless graphic design competitions open to the public, including students. Prizes can include money, equipment, jobs, and even scholarships.

Finding competitions to enter is pretty easy. In fact, a simple search on Google can generate several results. The following websites provide updated lists of competitions for several areas of graphic design:

- American Institute of Graphic Arts: www.aiga.org/competitions
- Contest Watchers: www.contestwatchers.com
- Dexigner: www.dexigner.com/design-competitions

different career goals in mind. And some students have discovered programs they either didn't know existed or were not initially interested in before they began their search for the right program.

EXTRACURRICULAR ACTIVITIES

Participating in extracurricular activities is a great way for high school and college students to gain experience and add credentials to their résumé. For high school students, being active outside of the classroom can be beneficial when it comes to applying to degree programs. Colleges and universities that have competitive admissions programs will take into account more than just an applicant's grades. Being involved in extracurricular activities and organizations can show admissions officers that a student is motivated, well-rounded, and responsible. Similarly, potential employers take involvement in organizations and clubs into consideration when interviewing and hiring.

There are many types of activities and organizations to get involved with, and several are directly relevant to graphic design careers. School newspapers and yearbooks, for

Young people entering the workforce may find it difficult to find a job if their résumé is empty. Participating in volunteer programs is one way to fill in blank space.

example, need individuals to lay out images and text before they can be published. Additionally, service projects and volunteer organizations, such as soup kitchens and park cleanups, are just a few of the many ways students can showcase themselves as active members of their local community.

ONLINE TRAINING RESOURCES

One of the many great benefits of having access to the web is the large number of training resources that are available to people who are interested in graphic design. Online courses that specialize in specific design programs are offered through several websites. Most of the training programs found online will not have an age restriction. However, it's important not to confuse online courses with degree programs offered by accredited colleges and universities. As much experience and skill as may be picked up from such courses, employers rarely consider them as a replacement for an actual degree. Nonetheless, online courses can help prospective graphic designers learn popular programs or pick up new tricks of the trade.

Aside from online classes and certification programs, there are numerous instructional videos that cover many aspects of design and design software. Lynda.com, for example, contains a wide variety of streaming videos that cover most aspects of each Adobe program. While Lynda.com charges a fee for access to its collection, it also provides the files that are used in the videos in order for the user to work alongside the instructor.

YouTube is another source for training resources. There are thousands of videos and channels that teach viewers the ins-and-outs of different design programs. The best part about YouTube is that the videos are free to watch. Furthermore, just using a search engine will turn up a vast number of web pages that give step-by-step instructions on how to perform different tricks with a specific program.

INTERNSHIPS

College students and recent graduates can have a tough

Internships are excellent ways to get real-world working experience in graphic design. A successful internship can even result in being hired as an employee.

time trying to find a job within the graphic design field. Many do not yet have the professional experience that employers often seek in applicants. During a troubled economy, the prospect of young people getting a job becomes even slimmer. Job seekers, both new and experienced, can end up spending months searching the web for job postings and writing countless cover letters that go unanswered.

One way to improve the odds of getting a job is to take up an internship. An internship is essentially a training position within a company. Graphic design interns may perform a variety of tasks for a business, perhaps working as an assistant for a team or directly under a manager or art director. Their duties can range from helping a designer create mock-ups for print to performing administrative tasks and errands. Additionally, some schools require their students to participate in internships. Compensation for an intern is generally up to the employer. Some employers pay their interns while others do not.

Employers often hire recent graduates who have internships listed on their résumés over those who do not. A 2013 employer survey conducted by the *Chronicle of Higher Education* and American Public Media's *Marketplace* indicates that there are several benefits associated with interning. The *Chronicle*'s research showed that internships were more important to employers than where an applicant went to school or even the applicant's grade point average.

Many companies use intern positions as a means of finding potential employees. If an intern performs well for a business, for example, there is a possibility the intern could be offered an actual staff position. According to 2012 statistics released by Internships.com, 69 percent of companies that employed one hundred or more people offered full-time positions to interns. Additionally, internships allow young people to determine whether or not they are making the right career choice.

There are several ways to find an internship in graphic design. Job forums and websites such as Craigslist.com and Mediabistro.com provide listings based on location and industry. Setting up an account on LinkedIn—a social network for professionals—is another option. Through LinkedIn, graphic design hopefuls can begin networking with professionals and businesses, showcase their designs, and discover internship opportunities. Also, a college or university may be able to assist students with finding internship programs. Finally, there is the old-fashioned method of picking up a phone and calling a business and asking. A successful internship is often the final stepping-stone that leads to a full-time job as a graphic designer.

chapter 5

Getting and Keeping Your First Job

J obs, unfortunately, do not simply fall from the sky. Even with a degree, talent, and internship experience, getting a job can take time. Unacknowledged applications and unreturned phone calls can, and should, be expected. For most young people, it will take a good amount of determination and hard work to find that first professional graphic design job.

Résumé and Cover Letter

The first step to finding a job for almost any professional career is writing a strong résumé and cover letter. These items are particularly important because they can determine the first and last impression a potential employer develops of an applicant. A hastily written cover letter that is littered with spelling errors, for example, may tell an employer that the writer lacks an eye for detail.

A résumé acts as a profile of one's education and work history—the story of "professional you." Though creating a résumé might sound boring, job applicants should work with the goal of demanding their audience's attention. Prospective employees should provide a detailed background of their education, including degree, graduation date, accomplishments, and organizational affiliations. Work history should be listed in chronological order and include job

CURRICULUM VITAE

Street Name. 1
70000 City Name
Tel: 0000 5555555
E-Mail: emailname@server.com

SUMMARY

- Experience in commercial engines development
- Expert knowledge in programming
- Strong experience in software design and architecture, animation, network programming, performance optimization
- 10 years of development experience. Worked on projects in various industries.
- Management of a small team of engineers

WORK EXPERIENCE

07/2007 - Present   Company Name Ltd. (United States)
Lead Position Name

Working on new innovative project

- Sed sed ipsum et tortor ornare ullamcorper nec quis orci.
- Suspendisse nec urna sit amet arcu volutpat imperdiet vitae et velit.
- Donec et ipsum interdum, vulputate augue eu, aliquam ipsum.
- Integer sed turpis tempus sem laoreet pellentesque vitae tincidunt diam.
- Maecenas mattis mauris non neque fermentum, vel gravida turpis dignissim.
- Aliquam rhoncus quam eu eros ullamcorper iaculis.

01/2005 – 07/2007   Company GmbH
Position Name

Worked mostly on engine development:

- Nulla non metus id neque tempor suscipit.
- Suspendisse bibendum elit et nulla euismod, vitae aliquet lectus accumsan.
- Nulla sed ipsum varius, imperdiet est malesuada, aliquam massa.
- Aliquam vitae enim sit amet velit consectetur gravida in et lacus

ACADEMIC QUALIFICATIONS

2005 – present   State Technical University
Post-graduate student. Doing research for dissertation

2004 – 2005   State Technical University
Master's degree in Computer Science

National University of Computer Science
Computer Science

A well-designed résumé is often the deciding factor in whether or not an individual gets an interview. It immediately shows an employer if a candidate has a basic understanding of effective layout.

duties and accomplishments. Descriptions of specific duties should be detailed and positive, highlighting one's skills and abilities. Additionally, a résumé should be visually appealing and not a mile long. Employers don't have time to read an entire book about each applicant.

A cover letter is a chance to give more details about an applicant, including goals and what the letter writer can bring to a company. The cover letter also gives an employer an example of a person's ability to communicate. Within the letter, applicants should tell the reader why they are interested in the employer and the specific position they are applying for, as well as how the applicant found out about the position. Most important, the letter should explain why the writer is the best match for the job. Giving examples from past experiences that relate to the job is helpful. Furthermore, the writer should avoid excess flattery when discussing the reader and the company overall. Focusing on how one would fit into the company environment and benefit the employer is the best move.

Putting Together a Portfolio

Graphic design is a visual profession where what you see is what you get. Employers rely

Unlike applicants in most other professions, a graphic designer needs to have a portfolio. A portfolio can contain professional and personal work that may interest an employer.

on visible proof that a potential designer possesses the qualities they are looking for in a worker. A portfolio functions as a designer's sales pitch, containing prints, sketches, and accompanying details with each sample piece. In itself, a portfolio is also a demonstration of a designer's aesthetic, or sense of beauty and art, as each piece should build off one another. With that in mind, a portfolio should not be thrown together quickly.

According to AIGA staff writer Steff Geissbuhler, "A well-structured portfolio has a beginning, a middle, and an end. It should be a well-designed book that shows off your work in the best possible light. Samples should be clean and removable. The sequence doesn't have to be chronological, but I wouldn't put early school work at the end. Don't forget that the final image leaves a more lasting impression than the first."

Employers often expect a portfolio review during an interview. Hard copies of one's work in a portfolio case are standard. But today's technology also allows for online portfolios, which are essentially websites that function the same as a physical portfolio. They contain the same materials within a visually appealing design that can be seen with the click of a button. For individuals who don't specialize in web design, creating an online portfolio should not be intimidating as there are several digital portfolio services that are easy to use, including Carbonmade and Dropbox.

JOB HUNTING

Finding a job has changed over the past few decades. In the past, people read the classified sections of newspapers. Today, job hunters spend their time navigating the web for employment opportunities and leads. Because of the competitive nature of the graphic design industry, searching for a job requires creativity, time, and effort to find prospective employers. Upon graduation, a person's college may be able to help him or her find an entry-level position within the graphic design industry. However, that luxury is not guaranteed to everyone, and so the job hunt begins.

Searching job forums and websites is a quick way to discover opportunities that match a person's talents. As is the case with finding internships, graphic design job listings can be found on various websites, including Craigslist and Mediabistro. For each job opportunity discovered, applicants should ensure that their cover letter and résumé are crafted for that particular

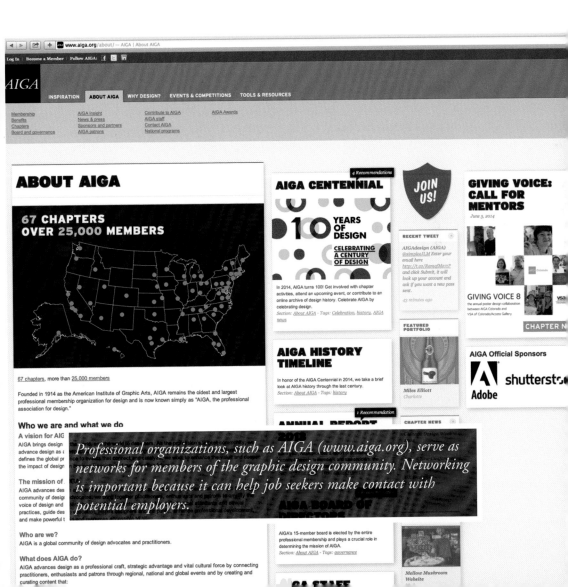

Professional organizations, such as AIGA (www.aiga.org), serve as networks for members of the graphic design community. Networking is important because it can help job seekers make contact with potential employers.

GRAPHIC DESIGN INDUSTRY OUTLOOK

Graphic designers face an uphill battle as they search for full-time employment. Unfortunately, there are many talented individuals who have an interest in graphic design and not enough positions for everyone. According to the U.S. Bureau of Labor Statistics, the employment of graphic designers is expected to grow slowly in the coming years. In fact, compared to all occupations, graphic design job growth is expected to be slower than average. The print industry, in particular, has experienced a significant loss of business as more work has moved to the web. By 2022, the Bureau of Labor Statistics predicts that graphic design jobs within newspaper, book, periodical, and directory publishers will decline 16 percent, rather than grow at all.

The slowdown in job growth can be attributed to a number of reasons. Nonetheless, there is good news to be found for graphic designers. The BLS also estimates that graphic design job growth within certain areas, including computer systems design, should grow. Because of the continuing growth of digital-related design, job seekers with web and mobile experience will have an advantage.

position and company. Writing letter after letter is time-consuming, but using a generic one for every opening will come off as . . . well, generic.

Networking is one of the most powerful tools for finding a job. Joining a design organization, such as AIGA, can be extremely valuable as it gives members the opportunity to interact with employers and employees within the industry.

Attending job fairs can also help graphic design hopefuls get in touch with companies that are hiring. Additionally, job seekers in the field can take advantage of social networks, such as LinkedIn, to find job openings and to introduce themselves to business recruiters for companies that are of interest. Upon meeting potential leads in person or online, be polite and share contact information. Keep in mind that if a company is not hiring today, that doesn't mean the company won't be looking for employees tomorrow, or at least the near future.

INTERVIEWING FOR A FIRST DESIGN JOB

Getting an interview can be hard work, and the hard work does not end once an applicant gets a phone call asking for him or her to come in for an interview. There are several things a person needs to keep in mind to make that hard-won interview a success.

Preparation is very important. This includes spending time beforehand researching the company with which one has the interview. Knowledge of the business shows an actual interest in the company's work and success, rather than simply a desire for a paycheck. Preparation also means applicants should have extra copies of their résumé and cover letter available, along with their portfolios.

Being on time for the interview is an absolute must. One of the worst mistakes applicants can make is showing up late for an interview. Studying one's travel route and accounting for the possibility of becoming slowed down by traffic will help assure a timely arrival. A person might also take a practice ride to the location for safe measure. Arriving too early to an interview can be problematic as well. Aim to arrive ten minutes early.

Dressing for success is another good rule of thumb when interviewing for a job. Nothing says "not hired" like a person coming to an interview wearing sandals and a T-shirt.

The job interview is the applicant's opportunity to make a great first impression on a potential employer. Interviews allow people to communicate what can not be easily summed up in a cover letter.

Depending on the company, consider wearing a suit or dress.

Finally, applicants would do well to just relax and be themselves. Shake hands with people and make eye contact during conversations. Avoid fidgeting and chewing gum. When discussing work, be sure to play up relevant experience and how it relates to the job opening at hand. Applicants should let the interviewer know that they have the ability to meet company expectations and more. At the end of the interview, thank them for their time.

STAYING COMPETITIVE AND CLIMBING THE LADDER

Getting a foot in the door of the graphic design industry is just the beginning of one's professional career. Once you have found an entry-level job, it is up to you to decide where to go from there. Through hard work, employees can eventually advance to higher positions, such as chief designer or art director.

They may even find themselves in charge of their own business one day.

Keep in mind, however, that the graphic design industry is not stationary. A large part of the graphic designer's job revolves around technology that is continually changing, improving, and becoming faster. In the 1990s, graphic designers may never have considered that many of the profession's jobs would eventually involve creating illustrations for games and apps that are used on the web and smartphones. Likewise, many professionals couldn't predict the decline of traditional printed newspapers and other businesses within the publishing industry.

As time goes by, the industry will continue to change, and with it the jobs and tools will also change. Knowing this, it is up to each individual to remain valuable within the graphic design profession. To do this, graphic designers must stay informed of trends in their field, in technology, and in business. Learning how to use new design software will keep designers in-step with the industry as older programs become obsolete. A continued desire to learn should help anyone find, and keep, their place as a graphic designer.

glossary

app An abbreviation for application, which is a small program, typically sold for mobile devices, that has a specific purpose.

branding Making a product or service memorable with consumers by using a similar design theme for advertising and marketing of the business.

browser A program used to navigate the web that can display coding such as HTML in a visual format.

certification Proof that official requirements to do a certain kind of work have been met.

computer-aided design (CAD) Using computer software to create, modify, and optimize 2-D and 3-D designs; commonly used for designing models and packaging for production.

desktop publishing Using a computer to create documents such as newspapers and brochures for printing or digital distribution.

draft A version of something that is created before the final version.

e-book A digital version of a book that is often read on tablets and smartphones.

entry-level The lowest position within the structure of a company.

infographic Representation of information, such as statistics, by using graphics that include charts, diagrams, or illustrations.

internship A program through which a student or other beginner gains practical, supervised experience in a professional field.

mock-up A draft of a design or arrangement of graphics and text that is to be printed.

multimedia Featuring a variety of digital media such as audio, video, and text.

networking Building professional relationships.

operating system Software that executes a computer's basic functions, such as opening and closing programs.

pixels Small dots that make up an image on a computer screen or display.

stylus A device shaped like a pen that is used to input drawings into a computer.

tablet A mobile computer that is contained within a single panel.

typography The arrangement of text with regards to style, size, and appearance.

user interface A program that allows a person to work easily with a computer.

for more information

American Institute of Graphic Arts (AIGA)
164 Fifth Avenue
New York, NY 10010
Website: http://www.aiga.org
(212) 807-1990
Founded in 1914, AIGA is a professional organization with
dozens of chapters and student groups across the United
States. The group works to connect members through
regional, national, and global events, including design
competitions and exhibitions.

Association of Registered Graphic Designers (RGD)
96 Spadina Avenue, Suite 210
Toronto, ON M5V 2J6
Canada
Website: http://www.rgd.ca
(888) 274-3688
This organization is a community for designers that promotes
sharing knowledge, research, continuous learning, and
mentorship. RGD hosts weekly online seminars and
events across Canada.

Graphic Artists Guild
32 Broadway, Suite 1114
New York, NY 10004
Website: http://www.graphicartistsguild.org
(212) 791-3400
Consisting of creative professionals and students, the Graphic
Artists Guild strives to equip members with education and
support to be competitive within the workforce.

International Council of Communication Design (Icograda)
455 Saint Antoine Ouest, Suite SS 10
Montreal, QC H2Z 1J1
Canada
Website: http://www.icograda.org
(514) 448-4949 ext. 221
Founded in 1963, Icograda is an international organization
    for professionals and organizations working within the
    communication design and expanded media industries.
    The organization works to promote research, education,
    and higher standards of design practice.

National Association of Photoshop Professionals (NAPP)
333 Douglas Road East
Oldsmar, FL 34677
Website: http://www.photoshopuser.com
With more than seventy-five thousand members
    internationally, NAPP is the largest digital graphics
    association. Specializing in informing and educating
    members on the Adobe line of design products, NAPP
    also publishes *Photoshop User Magazine.*

Organization of Black Designers (OBD)
300 M Street SW, Suite N110
Washington, DC 20024
Website: http://www.obd.org
OBD was established to increase the awareness of the contri-
    butions of African Americans to the graphic design
    profession. Members of OBD come from a variety of
    industries, including advertising, architectural, broadcast,
    and product design.

Society of Graphic Designers of Canada (GDC)
Arts Court, 2 Daly Avenue

Ottawa, ON K1N 6E2
Canada
Website: http://www.gdc.net
(877) 496-4453
GDC is an organization of professionals, educators, and
students across Canada. Through networking, events, and
publications, GDC works to promote and achieve high
standards of visual design and business practice in Canada.

WEBSITES

Because of the changing nature of Internet links, Rosen
Publishing has developed an online list of websites related to
the subject of this book. This site is updated regularly. Please
use this link to access the list:

http://www.rosenlinks.com/ECAR/Grap

for further reading

Airey, David. *Logo Design Love: A Guide to Creating Iconic Brand Identities.* Upper Saddle River, NJ: New Riders, 2009.

Baskinger, Mark, and William Bardel. *Drawing Ideas: A Hand-Drawn Approach for Better Design.* New York, NY: Watson-Guptill, 2013.

Bertling, Thomas. *How to Draw: Drawing and Sketching Objects and Environments from Your Imagination.* Culver City, CA: Design Studio Press, 2013.

Davies, Jo, and Derek Brazell. *Becoming a Successful Illustrator.* London, England: Fairchild Books, 2013.

Flath, Camden. *Media in the 21st Century: Artists, Animators, and Graphic Designers* (New Careers for the 21st Century: Finding Your Role in the Global Renewal). Broomall, PA: Mason Crest Publishers, 2010.

Freiberger, Paul. *When Can You Start? Ace the Interview and Get Hired.* Menlo Park, California: Career Upshift Productions, 2013.

Hagen, Rebecca, and Kim Golombisky. *White Space Is Not Your Enemy: A Beginner's Guide to Communicating Visually Through Graphic, Web & Multimedia Design.* 2nd ed. Waltham, MA: Focal Press, 2013.

Hannam, Ben. *A Graphic Design Student's Guide to Freelance.* Hoboken, NJ: Wiley, 2012.

Heller, Steven, and Lita Talarico. *Graphic: Inside the Sketchbooks of the World's Great Graphic Designers.* New York, NY: The Monacelli Press, 2010.

Heller, Steven, and Teresa Fernandes. *Becoming a Graphic Designer: A Guide to Careers in Design.* Hoboken, NJ: Wiley, 2010.

Heller, Steven, and Veronique Vienne. *100 Ideas That Changed Graphic Design*. London, England: Laurence King Publishing, 2012.

Kidd, Chip. *Go: A Kidd's Guide to Graphic Design*. New York, NY: Workman Publishing, 2013.

McWade, John. *Before & After: How to Design Cool Stuff*. San Francisco, CA: Peachpit Press, 2009.

Oleck, Joan. *Graphic Design and Desktop Publishing*. New York, NY: Rosen Publishing, 2010.

Palacio-Gomez, Bryony, and Armin Vit. *Graphic Design, Referenced: A Visual Guide to the Language, Applications, and History of Graphic Design*. Minneapolis, MN: Rockport Publishers, 2011.

Pease, Pamela. *Design Dossier: Graphic Design for Kids*. New York, NY: Paintbox Press, 2010.

Rothman, Julia, and Vanessa Davis. *Drawn In: A Peek into the Inspiring Sketchbooks of 44 Fine Artists, Illustrators, Graphic Designers, and Cartoonists*. London, England: Quarry Books, 2011.

Rowe, Robert, Gary Will, and Harold Linton. *Graphic Design Portfolio Strategies for Print and Digital Media*. Upper Saddle River, NJ: Pearson, 2009.

Sande, Warren, and Carter Sande. *Hello World! Computer Programming for Kids and Other Beginners*. Greenwich, CT: Manning Publications, 2009.

Seddon, Tony, and Jane Waterhouse. *Graphic Design for Nondesigners: Essential Knowledge, Tips, and Tricks, Plus 20 Step-by-Step Projects for the Design Novice*. San Francisco, CA: Chronicle Books, 2009.

Sherwin, David. *Creative Workshop: 80 Challenges to Sharpen Your Design Skills*. Palm Coast, FL: HOW Books, 2010.

Smith, Jennifer. *Adobe Creative Cloud Design Tools All-in-One for Dummies*. Hoboken, NJ: Wiley, 2013.

Taylor, Fig. *How to Create a Portfolio and Get Hired: A Guide for Graphic Designers and Illustrators.* 2nd ed. London, England: Laurence King Publishing, 2013.

White, Alex W. *The Elements of Graphic Design.* 2nd ed. New York, NY: Allworth Press, 2011.

Willenbrink, Mark, and Mary Willenbrink. *Drawing for the Absolute Beginner: A Clear & Easy Guide to Successful Drawing* (Art for the Absolute Beginner). New York, NY: North Light Books, 2006.

bibliography

Alani, Faisal. "Mac vs PC: Which Should I Buy?" ComputerWeekly.com, October 2010. Retrieved January 2014 (http://www.computerweekly.com/opinion/Mac -vs-PC-Which-should-I-buy).

Argent, Patrick. "Milton Glaser." *CSD Magazine*, August /September 1999. Retrieved December 2013 (http://www. aiga.org/interior.aspx?pageid=10631&id=11086).

Brin, Dinah Wisenberg. "Telecommuting Likely to Grow, Despite High-Profile Defections." Society for Human Resource Management, July 24, 2013. Retrieved December 2013 (http://www.shrm.org/hrdisciplines/ technology/articles/pages/telecommuting-likely-to -grow-bans.aspx).

Burnsed, Brian. "Degrees Are Great, but Internships Make a Difference." *U.S. News*, April 15, 2010. Retrieved February 2014 (http://www.usnews.com/education/ articles/2010/04/15/when-a-degree-isnt-enough).

Cantrell, Barry. Interview with author. December 20, 2014.

Creative Bloq. "20 Tips for Design Interview Success." CreativeBloq.com, November 13, 2012. Retrieved February 2014 (http://www.creativebloq.com/career/ design-interview-success-812255).

Edmonds, Rick, Emily Guskin, Amy Mitchell, and Mark Jurkowitz. "Newspapers: By the Numbers." State of the Media, May 7, 2013. Retrieved January 2014 (http:// stateofthemedia.org/2013/newspapers-stabilizing-but -still-threatened/newspapers-by-the-numbers).

Fischer, Karin. "A College Degree Sorts Job Applicants, but Employers Wish It Meant More." *Chronicle of Higher Education*, March 12, 2013. Retrieved February 2014 (http://chronicle.com/article/A-College-Degree-Sorts-Job/ 137625/#id=overview).

Geissbuhler, Steff. "Insights on Writing Your Résumé." AIGA.org. Retrieved February 2014 (http://www.aiga .org/resume-writing).

Geissbuhler, Steff. "Presenting Your Portfolio." AIGA.com. Retrieved February 2014 (http://www.aiga.org/portfolio -presenting).

Johnson, Joshua. "Are Print Designers Doomed? An Important Look at the Facts." DesignShack.net, July 18, 2011. Retrieved December 2013 (http://designshack.net/ articles/business-articles/are-print-designers-doomed-an -important-look-at-the-facts).

Johnson, Joshua. "Career Options: 10+ Types of Graphic Design Jobs to Consider." TheSiteSlinger.com, September 21, 2011. Retrieved December 2013 (http://thesiteslinger .com/blog/career-options-10-types-of-graphic-design -jobs-to/-consider).

Jones, Rhiannon. "Making an Internship Work." CreativeChoices, September 9, 2011. Retrieved February 2014 (http://www.creative-choices.co.uk/develop-your -career/article/making-an-internship-work).

Kaye, Gordon. "How Do Designers Feel About Print?" *Graphic Design Magazine*, 50th Anniversary survey. September 2013. Retrieved December 2013 (http:// www.gdusa.com/issue_2013/may/print_survey_feel_ print.php).

Poggenpohl, Sharon Helmer. "How to Select a Design School." AIGA.org, 1993. Retrieved February 2014 (http://www.aiga.org/guide-selectschool).

Poggenpohl, Sharon Helmer. "What Designers Need to Know." AIGA.org, 1993. Retrieved December 2013 (http://www.aiga.org/guide-designersneedknow).

Scott, Amy. "Internships Become the New Job Requirement."
   Marketplace.org, March 4, 2013. Retrieved February 2014
   (http://www.marketplace.org/topics/economy/education/
   internships-become-new-job-requirement).
Smith, Jacquelyn. "Internships May Be the Easiest Way to a Job
   in 2013." Forbes.com, December 12, 2012. Retrieved
   February 2014 (http://www.forbes.com/sites/jacquelynsmith/
   2012/12/06/internships-may-be-the-easiest-way-to-a-job
   -in-2013).
Sylvestre-Williams, Renee. "What Is Business Casual?" Forbes
   .com, May 9, 2012. Retrieved December 2013 (http://www
   .forbes.com/sites/reneesylvestrewilliams/2012/05/09/what-is
   -business-casual).
U.S. Bureau of Labor Statistics. "Graphic Designers."
   Occupational Outlook Handbook. Retrieved February 2014
   (http://www.bls.gov/ooh/arts-and-design/graphic-designers
   .htm#tab-6).
U.S. Bureau of Labor Statistics. "How to Become a Graphic
   Designer." *Occupational Outlook Handbook*. Retrieved
   February 2014 (http://www.bls.gov/ooh/arts-and-design/
   graphic-designers.htm#tab-4).

index

ABOUT THE AUTHOR

Joe Greek is a writer who has been obsessed with technology since elementary school. He has written for magazines, newspapers, and the web, covering topics that range from the stock market to web design. Additionally, he is a published author of technology-related books for young adults, including *Social Network–Powered Information Sharing* and *Writing Term Papers with Cool New Digital Tools.*

PHOTO CREDITS

Cover, p. 1 (figure) Andresr/Shutterstock.com; cover, p. 1 (background interior) Norman Chan/iStock/Thinkstock, (monitor screen) StudioM1/iStock/Thinkstock; pp. 4–5 Inga Ivanova/Shutterstock.com; pp. 8–9 scyther5/Shutterstock.com; pp. 10–11 Tyler McKay/Shutterstock.com; p. 15 Annette Shaff/Shutterstock.com; pp. 16–17, 28, 34–35 wavebreakmedia/Shutterstock.com; pp. 20, 30–31 Bloomberg/Getty Images; p. 25 blindfire/Shutterstock.com; pp. 26–27 Alan Klehr/Photodisc/Getty Images; p. 32 Syda Productions/Shutterstock.com; pp. 38, 56–57 Rhode Island School of Design; pp. 42–43 Hill Street Studios/Blend Images/Getty Images; pp. 44–45 sturti/E+/Getty Images; pp. 48–49 Photo Researchers/Getty Images; pp. 50–51 © AP Images; p. 55 Andrey Popov Shutterstock.com; p. 59 Courtesy of AIGA, www.aiga.org. Site design: Method, Inc. (New York, NY); pp. 62–63 Stephen Coburn/Shutterstock.com.

Designer: Matt Cauli; Editor: Jeanne Nagle; Photo Researcher: Marty Levick